THE ULTIMATE GUIDE TO
LIVING
YOUR
PURPOSE

THE ULTIMATE GUIDE TO
LIVING
YOUR
PURPOSE

---

7 STEPS TO CREATING THE
Life You Crave

SHAWN R. MCLEOD

THE ULTIMATE GUIDE TO LIVING YOUR PURPOSE
ISBN: 978-0-9827035-0-2
Printed in the United States of America
© 2013 by Shawn R. McLeod -- Revised, 2015
Shawn R. McLeod
email: shawn@LivingYourPurpose.org
website: www.LivingYourPurpose.org

Unless otherwise noted, all Scripture quotations are from the New King James Version of the Holy Bible. Copyright © 1979, 1980, 1982 by Thomas Nelson, Inc., publishers. Used by permission. Scripture quotations marked KJV are from the King James Version of the Bible. Scripture taken from THE MESSAGE. Copyright © 1993, 1994, 1995, 1996, 2000, 2001, 2002. Used by permission of NavPress Publishing Group. Scripture quotations taken from the Amplified® Bible, Copyright © 1954, 1958, 1962, 1964, 1965, 1987 by The Lockman Foundation. Used by permission. (www.Lockman.org)

Although the author and publisher have made every effort to ensure the accuracy and completeness of information contained in this book, we assume no responsibility for errors, inaccuracies, omissions, or any inconsistency herein. Any slights of people, places, or organizations are unintentional.

ATTENTION CORPORATIONS, UNIVERSITIES, COLLEGES, AND PROFESSIONAL ORGANIZATIONS: Quantity discounts are available on bulk purchases of this book for educational, or gift purposes. For information, or to schedule books signings or speaking engagements please contact the author at: shawn@LivingYourPurpose.org

Cover Design by Adjayceency at 99Designs.com

DEDICATION

To my Lord and Savior, Jesus Christ! I praise the Lord for the wisdom He has shared with me to help expand the Kingdom of God on Earth. It is a privilege and honor to receive and communicate these lessons to His people in whatever media or format He requires.

Without the support of my loving family, this work could not have been possible. I thank the Lord for my husband, Sherman, who is my protector and confidante. He is indeed a God-given gift who helps me to daily walk in my destiny as he is our family's visionary, leader, and teacher. And, to our children Jerome, DeShawn, and Sherman Ernest, thanks for believing in me. To my mom, Delores, my first cheerleader and mentor who covers our family in prayer. To my sister Shelby, for being my very first intercessor, the younger defending the older. To Tim, Timmy and Nylah, Sam, Patty, Simone, and Samuel, thank you for your love and prayers.

To my pastor, Bishop David G. Evans of Bethany Baptist Church, whose faithfulness propelled me into my purpose, which is writing about Kingdom principles to share with God's people. He conducted an entrepreneurship course during 2010-2011 called the *Kingdomaires*. It was during this class that I constructed my very first vision board. And vision boarding is a key strategy for discovering your God-ordained purpose as detailed in this book.

To Nicole Irene Gay, whose *I Want to Be An Author* workshop I attended in 2010. Her mentorship and drive were the original impetus and motivation to get me started writing.

Also, to Reverend Niki Brown, one of the coordinators of Bethany's Women's Ministry who believed in me enough to allow me to present my first purpose vision discovery workshop to the women of the Career Empowerment Network.

When an endeavor like writing your first book is undertaken, it requires midwives to complete the birthing process. Thanks to the Women of the "DGG" Organization for your prayers, intercession, and encouragement: Jackie, Katrina, and Teresa. Most dear friends, fellow Drexel graduates, and accountability partners, may the Lord bless you as richly as you have blessed me. Thank you for strengthening me during my journey of purpose discovery.

The Lord always brings the right resources in just the right timing to His assignments. What a pleasure it has been working with two enormously talented consultants and editors: Dr. Patricia Powell and Nicole O'Dell! I do so appreciate your expertise, diligence and enthusiasm.

CONTENTS

ILLUSTRATIONS

EXERCISES

INTRODUCTION

This book is for those who have reached a point in their lives where not only is it time for a career change, but, you're ready to do something about it. You might be retired, but feeling unfulfilled and bored, fearing that you've missed your prime time to impact the world. Or, perhaps you're trying to decide what you want to be when you *grow up* and have no idea where to start the journey of finding out.

Welcome to **The Ultimate Guide to Living Your Purpose:** *7 Steps to Creating the Life You Crave!* This work is divided into three parts. **Part 1** contains the methodology I have used to successfully understand my purpose and help others with their purpose discovery journey.

Part 2 details how to apply the seven-step purpose vision process. In the end, you will see a picture of your purpose both as it has developed to this point, and where you are going in the not too distant future. You'll find out how to use vision boarding, journaling, and scrapbooking to **WRITE YOUR PURPOSE VISION** and make it clear so you can use it to map out your future with the help of the Holy Spirit. You will be able to easily explain it to others, especially those called to be a resource to you in achieving your purpose.

Part 3 provides additional resources that you will find useful, including answers to Frequently Asked Questions, Purpose Prayers, and Digital Image Links.

As you read and apply these concepts, you will have powerful tools to help you not only discover, but hone your purpose through this revelatory, iterative process.

This resource is the tool kit you need to:

- Find your true, God-ordained purpose;
- Fulfill the destiny that your Divine Designer has planned for you; and
- Understand that your true destiny is not attained apart from help from your Divine Designer, and His Holy Spirit.

I would enjoy hearing your feedback. If you would like help along the way, reach out to me at: shawn@LivingYourPurpose.org. You can submit your email address and be added to our email list. You will receive important updates and advance notice about upcoming tele-seminars and workshops. Consultations are available upon request.

PART 1:
LIVING YOUR
GOD-ORDAINED PURPOSE

CHAPTER 1 - LIVING YOUR TRUE PURPOSE

What Is Your True Purpose?

Your purpose was established from the beginning of time. It is in your very DNA, the Lord having knit you together in your mother's womb. The passage in Psalms 139:13-16 sums up how long ago the Lord had been thinking of you and forming you even before your birth. The Bible says we are *marvelously made*. He designed your personality, your looks, your talents, your gifts, even the era when you would be born, as well as your birth order and family.

YOU ARE MARVELOUSLY MADE!

Psalms 139:13-16 The Message Translation (EMPHASIS ADDED)

Oh yes, you shaped me first inside, then out; You formed me in my mother's womb.

I thank you, High God—you're breathtaking!
Body and soul, **I am marvelously made!**

I worship in adoration—what a creation!

> You know me inside and out, you know every bone in my body; You know exactly how I was made, bit by bit, how I was sculpted from nothing into something.
>
> Like an open book, you watched me grow from conception to birth; all the stages of my life were spread out before you,
>
> The days of my life all prepared before I'd even lived one day.

When you don't understand your purpose, there's an aimlessness to your life that seems incurable and inescapable. You feel the need to wander, looking for meaning and value. Deep seated unhappiness and discontent prevails. You go about life doing as only you see fit, living for your own selfish desires, or oblivious to the fact that your life has true meaning and destiny.

Your true calling is that thing you were created to do, born to do—that assignment no one else in the universe can accomplish. In fact, you were designed with a specific intent. You are not to go about your daily lives ignorant of it. It's something you're driven to seek and will not find true comfort and rest until you're walking in it with the people you were ordained to share it.

Your true, God-ordained purpose is something to be discovered. It is not revealed all at once. It is opened like the petals of a flower, little by little. It is revealed layer by layer, grown into. It comes in phases as your maturity level dictates.

Mentors seem to appear when you are ready to receive them, as if you're being guided down the path with carefully dropped breadcrumbs to lead you on to the next step at the exact time. The right counselors and teachers help you improve in understanding and capability, pushing you from phase to phase as you achieve promotion. It's an exciting journey of self-discovery, often requiring turmoil and chaos to birth its different aspects.

My Purpose Discovery Journey

Very early in life, we begin to notice the things that set us apart, the things that make us unique. Our talents and gifts come to the fore. I've always loved to write, so it was natural when, as a teen, I took up journaling. It was a way for me to capture my thoughts on paper. Writing was a common thread throughout my life. It plays into my purpose because it is a skill I use in my day job now, but, it is also a passion of mine.

To differentiate purpose vs. destiny, **purpose** is defined as the reason the Lord made us, but **destiny** is lived out according to our daily life choices. Even in the season of a wrong job, He is achieving His purpose in us because his objective is maturity and dependence on Him. I write because I really enjoy it. I would do it whether or not someone paid me to do it.

As I got older, I began to realize my purpose was multifaceted. It manifested in several arenas: my home-life, career, and integral relationships. In college, when I met and later married my husband, I understood that our union was part of our dual destiny. Choosing the right life partner was critical, as our destinies would become intertwined forever. As parents, we were a pivotal part of our children's destiny and purpose. And part of our responsibility as parents was helping our children achieve their purposes.

After working for many years in a corporate job, I decided to get a Master of Business Administration (M.B.A.) degree. It was another stepping stone in honing my understanding of my true purpose. That journey came to a critical point in March, 2009. It was a very stressful time in my life. Working full time, going to school, and managing my role as a wife and mom required critical life-balancing skills that were difficult to manage. Thank God for my husband's constant willingness to share the burden of raising a young family and always bringing a mature perspective.

I had always enjoyed learning, and graduate school was no exception. But, toward the end of the degree program, I was having trouble completing my M.B.A. thesis, having missed some key required milestone dates for chapter submissions. No matter what I tried, I couldn't unearth inspiration to write at all. It was very frustrating, and I had come too far to mess up at the end.

I saw an advertisement for a Ministers and Missions conference being conducted by Dr. Bill Winston, founder and pastor of Living Word Christian Center in Oak Park, Illinois. Dr. Winston had gathered several dynamic speakers I wanted to hear including Dr. Cindy Trimm, author, entrepreneur, best-known for her writing and teaching on the art of strategic prayer, and, Dr. Lance Wallnau, teacher and speaker whose name has become synonymous with the Seven Mountains of Influence. [i]

The conference theme was *Manifesting the Sons of God*. Although I wanted to go, I had made no plans to get there because completing my thesis was my

---

[i] Hillman, O. (n.d.). *7 cultural mountains*. Retrieved from http://www.7culturalmountains.org

priority. My research project was due just days before the conference was scheduled to begin.

The Spirit of the Lord kept impressing upon me to make flight and hotel arrangements to attend the conference. This spiritual push was unusual and had not happened before in this manner. I would be sitting at the kitchen table staring at the computer trying to write. I made all sorts of excuses about not going to the conference, such as the lack of funds, work responsibilities, and family commitments. The Holy Spirit was hearing none of my excuses. Never before had I felt such insistent pressure.

When I finally booked my flight and made hotel reservations, I found that I was able to get some sentences onto the electronic page. Wow, what obedience can do for your writing! My writing flow returned, and I was able to get everything done for my M.B.A. thesis' electronic submission within minutes of the final deadline. Phew!

My husband was very supportive of my going to the conference, even though my decision seemed out of the blue.   I was getting more and more excited. My expectations for the trip were high because of all the Lord had done to get me there. As I traveled there, my spirit was vibrating with anticipation.

At the conference, as I heard the material the speakers had prepared, I couldn't write fast enough to keep up with all I heard. Dr. Cindy Trimm's words resonated with me. I was certainly on the verge of true breakthrough!

Dr. Trimm's sermon topic was titled *Birthed Out!* It was based upon John 3:1-7 where Nicodemus, a Jewish leader, visited Jesus at night, asking how he could see the kingdom. Dr. Trimm captured the essence of what I had been working in my personal studies. I had not before grasped the full picture. Here's the scripture passage:

YOU MUST BE RECREATED TO ENTER INTO KINGDOM DESTINY

John 3:1-7 The Message Translation (EMPHASIS ADDED)

1-2 There was a man of the Pharisee sect, Nicodemus, a prominent leader among the Jews. Late one night he visited Jesus and said, "Rabbi, we all know you're a teacher straight from God. No one could do all the God-pointing, God-revealing acts you do if God weren't in on it." **3** Jesus said, "You're absolutely right. Take it from me: **Unless a person is born from above, it's not possible to see what I'm pointing to—to God's kingdom.**" **4** "How can anyone," said Nicodemus, "be born who has already been born and grown

---

> up? You can't re-enter your mother's womb and be
> born again. What are you saying with this 'born-
> from-above' talk?" **5-6** Jesus said, "You're not
> listening. Let me say it again. **Unless a person
> submits to this original creation**—the 'wind-
> hovering-over-the-water' creation, the invisible
> moving the visible, a baptism into a new life—**it's
> not possible to enter God's kingdom**. When
> you look at a baby, it's just that: a body you can
> look at and touch. But the person who takes shape
> within is formed by something you can't see and
> touch—the Spirit—and becomes a living spirit.

The essence of Dr. Trimm's message for me that
evening was three-fold:

- Rebirth, or baptism into a new life (v.5-6)
  was a prerequisite to kingdom revelation,
  understanding and access. That new birth,
  which for me occurred when I was born again
  so many years before, connected me to my
  God-ordained, kingdom purpose.

- Part of my God-ordained purpose was being
  served in my current job.

- Serving God as part of His kingdom
  connected me to kingdom resources and to
  my power to get wealth.

Provision was already made for me to access, see, and understand my kingdom assignment. I didn't have to look any further to find it. All the rights and privileges had already been granted, after my taking that first step of rebirth. I had vastly overcomplicated it.

Part of my purpose was being served in my current job. My job was my assignment in the Kingdom of God. The Lord had planted me there in preparation for a time and season that had not yet appeared. But, I was working for Him. I was to follow His timetable. I was being groomed and needed to grow and mature both in my walk with Him as well as in technical skills, communications skills, and relationship-building skills.

This was not how I had seen things previously, which led to much frustration, since I was ready to move on to another opportunity in the company, and had been for some time. All I could sense in my spirit was that transition was about to occur. It took a long while to birth, but the Lord was readying me for the challenges to come.

At the same time, He was preparing the territory I was to take, moving and shifting people and circumstances to achieve His will. It is all hard to see when you think of it in the daily happenings, as opposed to the big picture. His ways are indeed higher than our ways, His thoughts higher than our thoughts. (Isaiah 55:9) It takes us a while to see all He's working out.

The "power to get wealth" (Deuteronomy 8:18) was already within my grasp, right where I was in His will. My purpose was not somewhere afar off awaiting some proper lever to be pulled. I thought that changing jobs or even changing companies would automatically lead to greater fulfillment and more money. I was wrong.

Also, I had been giving at my church, sowing seeds in various ministries with an expectation for a financial harvest. I was expecting that my harvest was to come back in kind on my timetable. That it would appear on my doorstep, come to me mysteriously in the mail, or drop from the sky. How wrong I was!

In fact, the Lord has indeed already given me the power to get wealth. That wealth is in kingdom ideas, innovations, insights, strategies, and technologies. Ideas that He dropped in my spirit were to be executed without fail, right where I was! These kingdom ideas were sources of income, and He would provide the resources for me to accomplish His assignments. These opportunities were indeed located at my day job as well as in business ideas and resources which He had given to my husband and me to implement as entrepreneurs.

The next night of the conference, Dr. Lance Wallnau, opened my eyes to the revelation of the *Seven Mountains of Influence* as originally identified by Bill Bright. Dr. Wallnau explained that the Kingdom of God is firmly established in the Earth within the seven mountains of influence.

The Seven Mountains of influence in culture are:

1. Religion
2. Family
3. Education
4. Government
5. Media and Communications
6. Art and Entertainment
7. Business and Finance

There is a battle in the earth for these seven mountains. They are being fought over by the righteous dwellers of the Kingdom of God and the strongholds of darkness. These mountains are to be taken for the Kingdom of God. They are akin to a Christian's modern day *Promised Land*, which the children of Israel were to take from their enemies. This was land that the Lord had already given them. (Joshua 3:9-11).

Today, they represent world systems and nations which must be taken back and dominated for Christ's Kingdom. I also learned that my God-ordained purpose had a location in one or several of these mountains. I needed to use Kingdom tools and strategies to dominate my assigned mountains using my divinely given gifts and talents. **Essentially, the whole world awaits the *Manifestation of the Sons of God*. This happens as they take their places in their assigned purpose.**

My understanding is still growing regarding the seven mountains concept. God is still revealing the details of His reason for getting me to Living Word Christian Center in March, 2009. However, nothing just happens. To this day, I believe I was strongly directed to attend the conference to hear the Word that these two dynamic thought leaders were to deliver. It was critical for me to connect with lifetime mentors who had words of life for my family and me.

I had to leave my comfort zone to hear and grasp concepts that were going to revolutionize my thinking. Prior to that, I wasn't sure why I was born into the roles I filled, or why my gifts and talents were constructed as they were.

Growing restless, I had been working at the same company for eight years in the same job. It always felt as if there was so much more to my life than I was living in my career. Two engineering degrees and an M.B.A. just seemed like a good set of nice-to-haves, creating entree' to my present position, but only taking me so far. I was hungry for greater understanding. But, had I moved on prematurely, I would have missed or delayed the discovery of my calling.

Each of us has a story of purpose discovery. If you can't tell your story, perhaps you haven't yet discovered your true, God-ordained kingdom purpose. The twists and turns that lead to our grasping it are as individual as we are. The more I talk with people about their discovery journey, the more I want to help others take the much needed steps to understand and take hold of their God-ordained purpose.

The pages of this book contain the truths and the tools that have helped me. Vision boarding is a strategic part of this process. In Part 1 of this book, I explain ways the Lord has taught me to better understand my purpose and how to grow into it. Part 2 is constructed to teach you how to use the vision boarding tools and exercises to map your unique pathway.

Your Goals vs. Submission to God

There is a distinct difference between a purpose you design vs. one that is linked to and achieved because of your repositioning in Christ through the new birth.
There is a constant struggle in us regarding who's will to follow, yours or God's. To obtain your God-ordained purpose, you must make His desires more important than your own. Psalm 37:4 admonishes us to delight ourselves in the Lord, and as a result He makes our desires align with His. But it's not a one-time thing. It's a daily process of surrender and renewal.

You were born with gifts and talents which enable you to accomplish many things. Only you can make the decision to use your gifts for the Lord. Imagine that it is possible to waste those gifts and talents in pursuit of your will, like the Prodigal Son in Luke 15:11-18. He made a decision to obtain his inheritance early in order to pursue his destiny apart from the Father, and was later brought to ruin.

We have been admonished to honor the Lord with our substance in Proverbs 3:9-10. When we honor the Lord first with our gifts and talents, we really do gain our heart's desire. There is a promised reward for that surrender as stated in verse 10...Provision! His provision is not just for personal consumption, but for taking possession of our assigned mountains and helping others do the same.

HONOR THE LORD FIRST AND FOREMOST

Prov 3:9-10 KJV(Emphasis Added)
9 Honour the Lord with thy **substance**, and with the firstfruits of all thine increase:
10 So shall thy barns be filled with plenty, and thy presses shall burst out with new wine.

What is meant by *substance*? The scriptures reference our tangible goods when the word substance is used in the King James version. It is the word CHAYIL in Hebrew which means our strength, wealth, military might, or ability. The following table shows some examples of how the word substance is used in the bible.

WHAT IS SUBSTANCE?

DEFINITIONS	REFERENCES
Goods, food, jewelry, clothing	"And also that nation, whom they shall serve, will I judge: and afterward shall they come out with great substance" Gen. 15:14
What you have accomplished with your work; the fruit of your thinking and problems you have solved	"Bless, Lord, his substance, and accept the work of his hands..." Deut. 33:11
That which you own as a result of employing your gifts and talents.	"His [Job's] substance also was seven thousand sheep, and three thousand camels, and five hundred yoke of oxen, and five hundred she asses, and a very great household; so that this man was the greatest of all the men of the east." Job 1:3

According to Proverbs 3:9-10, we are to honor the Lord with that which is important to us, including our time. This kind of sacrifice honors the Lord. It shows that we value Him and His direction more than we value our own desires.

Our Reasonable Sacrifice

Not only are we to commit our substance to the Lord, He requires our entire being. He calls that sacrifice our reasonable service. This is a passage from the book of Romans, chapter 12. Compare the KJV and Message Translations.

WE ARE TO BE A LIVING, DAILY SACRIFICE

Romans 12:1-2 KJV (Emphasis Added)
12 I beseech you therefore, brethren, by the mercies of God, that ye **present your bodies a living sacrifice**, holy, acceptable unto God, which is your reasonable service.
2 And be not conformed to this world: but be ye transformed by the renewing of your mind, that ye may prove what is that good, and acceptable, and perfect, will of God.

Romans 12:1-2:
The Message Translation (Emphasis Added)
So here's what I want you to do, God helping you: **Take your everyday, ordinary life - your sleeping, eating, going-to-work, and walking-around life - and place it before God as an offering.** Embracing what God does for you is the best thing you can do for him. 2 Don't become so well-adjusted to your culture that you fit into it without even thinking. Instead, fix your

---

attention on God. You'll be changed from the inside out. Readily recognize what he wants from you, and quickly respond to it. Unlike the culture around you, always dragging you down to its level of immaturity, God brings the best out of you, develops well-formed maturity in you.

It becomes difficult to carry out this personal sacrifice when we place other things ahead of our relationship with the Lord. In fact, this passage is not a request but a command. It should be considered a prerequisite to understanding your purpose.

The second verse in the Message translation is very compelling. It speaks about how we must change our thinking so that God can bring out the best in us, including the maturity we need to walk in the purpose for which we have been designed.

CHAPTER 2 - THE LORD'S PURPOSE FOR YOU: THE END GAME

As a person of God-ordained purpose, you must view your life beyond the current, day-to-day ups and downs. There is a definite, identifiable pattern to the events of your life. When you view these life events as disjointed happenings, you feel happy when things are going well and sad when things are upside down.

But, be encouraged and do not lose heart! Why? This is a test of your faith--this difficulty, this challenge, this tragedy. In James 1:2-4, the challenge is made very clear. The **End Game** is in verse 4: "that ye may be perfect and entire wanting nothing." Compare it in the Message translation: "**Let it do its work so you become mature and well-developed, not deficient in any way**".

THE END GAME

James 1:2-4 KJV
(EMPHASIS ADDED)
2 My brethren, count it all joy when you fall into divers temptations;
3 Knowing this, that the trying of your faith worketh patience.
4 But, let patience have her perfect work, **that ye may be perfect and entire wanting nothing.**

James 1:2-4 The Message Translation
(EMPHASIS ADDED)
2-4 Consider it a sheer gift, friends, when tests and challenges come at you from all sides. You know that under pressure, your faith-life is forced into the open and shows its true colors. So don't try to get out of anything prematurely. **Let it do its work so you become mature and well-developed, not deficient in any way.**

Understanding this key concept is revolutionary in that it makes the point of why things happen as they do. There are times in your life when the onslaught of the enemy seems overwhelming and frustration levels are very high. You find yourself questioning the merits of continuing to push forward. This is when **Endurance** is flagging and **Spiritual Energy** is waning. But, both your endurance and spiritual energy need to be in high gear to continue on the journey toward your purpose.

Satan wishes to keep you from your destiny. In fact his mission is to steal, kill, and destroy all God has for you. (John 10:10) But he has no power to thwart God's plan unless you give it to him. He can cause delays and detours by causing your stumbling with temptations to sin. You stumble when you're lured away by temptations or disobedience. Your endurance is de-energized when you fail to resist. However, your endurance is strengthened and revitalized when you successfully resist temptation.

Spiritual endurance is built when:

- you successfully pass the Lord's Faith Tests or trials, and
- you successfully resist a Temptation to sin from Satan.

The Lord tests or tries your faith to help you grow and mature in Him. Each time you pass a test of your faith from the Lord, your endurance is increased and your patience during trials is greatly improved. However, Satan, who goes about like a roaring lion seeking whom he may devour and divert from purpose, uses temptation as a weapon against you. But, rest assured that God does not tempt men to sin. He Himself cannot be tempted with sin and never tempts us. (James 1:13)

Endurance Building: Faith, Temptation and Purpose

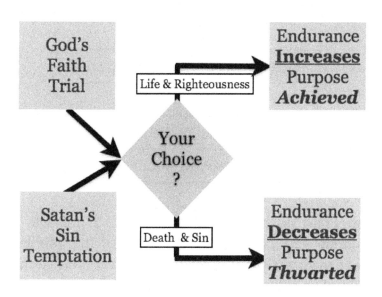

See the **Endurance Building Diagram**. Your faith on trial seeks to answer one question: *Will you believe God's Word or not?* He has given us His promises to stand upon. We get to choose whether we accept them as the truth. "Let God be true and every man a liar!" (Romans 3:4)

Now Satan, on the other hand, seeks to lure us off course to thwart our God-ordained purpose. During our trials, tribulations, and afflictions, he presents these ungodly opportunities to disbelieve what God says about us, or what He has told us to do.

There are three main temptation categories which can be combined in any way:

Satan's Temptation Categories
The Lust of the Flesh
The Lust of the Eyes
The Pride of Life

The **Trial** is the specific scenario God presents to examine our faith in His Word. It's the problem couched in a situation designed to show you certain areas of your life and character, and whether there is a need to improve and mature.

The **Test** is the presentation of a choice or question. Your spiritual endurance is either energized and built up or de-energized, depending on your choices in these various situations. As you successfully go through the tests of your faith and resist temptation, your spiritual muscles grow under the stress.

For example, let us go to Adam and Eve in the Garden of Eden in Genesis, chapter three. The couple is enticed by the serpent to eat of the Tree of the Knowledge of Good and Evil by the question: "**Yea, hath God said, Ye shall not eat of every tree of the garden?**"

The trial, "Yea, hath God said", reveals Eve's penchant to doubt the words of God which she knew very well and had been observing for some time (Genesis 3:3). The **Pride of Life** temptation category is demonstrated in Eve's entertaining the thought that the Lord had misled her and deciding to believe the lie rather than God the Father. Then she looked at the forbidden fruit noting it was good to look at: **Lust of the Eyes**. When she took and ate of the fruit and gave her husband, that was the **Lust of the Flesh.** And so the fall of man ensued.

Well, Satan's tactics have not changed and are used against us today. If we take the time to examine the instances of testing in our lives we can clearly see them. The question is: Will we allow either fiery trials from the Lord or temptations from Satan to thwart our God-ordained purpose? The answer is a resounding, "No!"

Remember, we have the following provisions to overcome temptations:

- When temptations come, God limits them to what we can successfully endure. (I Corinthians 10:13)
- The Lord always provides a way of escape and is always present to see you are aware of that way. (I Corinthians 10:13)
- You can pray that you do not enter into temptations. (Matthew 6:13)
- You can depend on the Word of God to lead you to the correct decision, delivering you from the evil one.

When you successfully resist Satan's lies your endurance is increased. Each success leads to more success. One promotion leads to another. See the following **Endurance Growth** chart.

Impacts to Endurance Levels

Each success takes you from one endurance level to the next higher endurance level. Eventually, you can believe God for anything. You will stretch more readily beyond your comfort zone and experience victories for God!

Endurance Level Progression

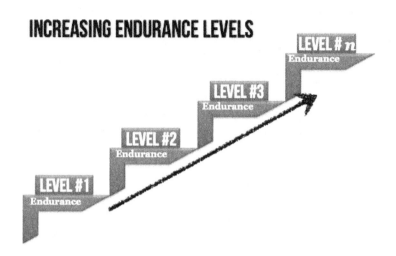

The Lord's objective is to get you to grasp a scriptural promise which directly relates to your current problem(s). Your taking hold of His promises leads to His provision. The Lord is always faithful and true to His Word. Thus, we need to understand how to consistently pass the Lord's exams as we proceed through life. The question is: What is required to pass a trial of your faith?

There is one thing that brings the Lord great pleasure, and that is to be believed. (Hebrews 11:6) His desire for His children is that they believe His promises, take Him at His word, so as to literally move mountains. That is my constant personal goal.

> **OUR FAITH PLEASES GOD TREMENDOUSLY**
>
> **Hebrews 11:6 (KJV)**
> But **without faith, it is impossible to please him**: for he that cometh to God must believe that he is, and that he is a rewarder of them that diligently seek him.

The scriptures are full of God's promises to us. We can scoop up any one of them and choose to meditate on it and allow it to transform our thinking and, more importantly, our actions.

Challenges Lead to Self-Discovery

When God's promise is believed, as we encounter challenges, what previously seemed insurmountable can now be overcome. Our success is well within reach. It will take time, energy, and focus to achieve it.

God's Word is the battering ram that breaks down road blocks and barriers to our purpose. It adds the spring to our steps, pushing us to clear life's hurdles like an Olympic gold-medal hurdler. Our awareness of this principle gets us successfully through the problem and on to achieving purpose.

Purpose Discovery Equips Us

THE WINDING ROAD TO PURPOSE

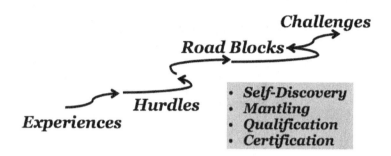

The size of the struggle and our attitude during the transition is critical. The larger the obstacle, the greater our faith must be. But, also, the larger problem, the larger the provision and resource for our battle, and the greater the reward. With God, we are always victorious!

As we continue to progressively pass each faith trial, there is promotion and certification. Our mantle, or territory of responsibility and authority can be increased. When we discover that our capability is increasing, we qualify for greater and greater challenges. You will notice that your intimacy with the Lord becomes more and more critical!

Progressive Intimacy with Him

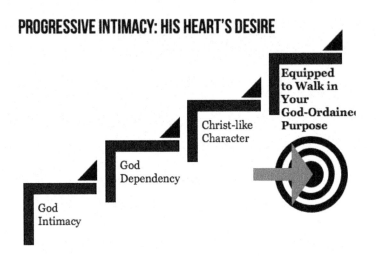

PROGRESSIVE INTIMACY: HIS HEART'S DESIRE

Equipped to Walk in Your God-Ordaineᵈ Purpose

Christ-like Character

God Dependency

God Intimacy

There are three basic things the Lord desires to see in His relationship with you:

- Intimacy
- Dependency
- His Image and Likeness

As we progress upward in our journey of greater intimacy with Him, we become equipped with the much greater strength and abilities required to walk in our God-ordained purpose. Improving this relationship to the point where we have been prepared to take on our true assignment is His ultimate equipping method.

In everything that happens in your life, the Lord
promises that He will never leave you nor turn away
from you. He has promised that during the ups and
downs of your life, you will not be alone. In this
knowledge, you can take comfort. And, in spite of the
prickliness of our personality, He remains in close
proximity to encourage and sustain us. He has given
us His Word to aid in transforming our worldly
thinking. Even in our often unlovable state, He
remains close, confirming His love for us, standing by
to offer strength and encouragement. He has made us
with an innate need for companionship with Him.

We were constructed with the innate desire to
worship the Lord. Even when we choose not to
worship Him, we will end up worshipping and serving
something or someone because that is how we are
made. Living distracted, busy, frustrated lives absent
from His peace is our choice.

His love for us is impossible to fully comprehend. But,
as we come to know Him we come to depend upon His
presence and His guidance as a lifeline. You may have
had a human friend with whom you have made a
connection that lasted a lifetime. It is said that long-
married couples start looking like one another.
Eventually, we will look and act just like our Heavenly
Father. We take on His image and likeness. The
required transformation begins to occur. It is

awesome to see how the Lord works out all the details in getting us there! We only find the game plan details as we seek Him in earnest.

GOD HAS WONDERFUL PLANS FOR US!

Jeremiah 29:11-12 (KJV)
For I know the plans I have for you, says the Lord. They are plans for good and not for evil, to give you a future and a hope. In those days when you pray, I will listen. You will find me when you seek me, **if you look for me in earnest.**

Our journey is made significantly easier when we have Someone to guide our every move. We need comfort and encouragement when it looks like we won't make it, or when we just plain mess up. The Holy Spirit has been given to us to play that role. Not only is He our personal guide in all the Lord requires, but also our secret weapon.

CHAPTER 3 - THE HOLY SPIRIT: OUR SECRET WEAPON AND GUIDE

By now, you have discovered God's end game for you and how your walk through a series of tests and temptations increases your endurance and tightens your relationship with Him. If it all looks overwhelming, know that you have the best kind of help. The Holy Spirit is our secret weapon and guide!

The reason I use the words "secret weapon" is that the Holy Spirit is the most powerful being in the universe. Because He is spirit, He is invisible to the physical eye.

When you accept Jesus as Lord of your life, the Holy Spirit will reside within your recreated spirit. Only then can your spiritual ears clearly hear Him. He is within you fighting internal battles to help you think and believe right. The Holy Spirit helps you to war against external spiritual enemies. All of this is available to you as a son or daughter of God.

REQUIREMENT FOR BEING LED IS SONSHIP

Romans 8:14
For as many as are led by the Spirit of God, they are the sons of God.

Finding your individual, God-ordained purpose can only be accomplished with the Holy Spirit's direction and guidance. Romans 8:14 promises that when you are part of God's family, that is a son or daughter, you will be led to your purpose. The Lord's instructions are specific and personal.

It's a daily walk of acknowledging His leading and Lordship. You desire more and more to connect with Him. Listening for His voice and following His leading makes us successful. ***Remember that the Holy Spirit is not God at our service, but, we are in His service.***

Also, it is the Holy Spirit who gives us the power to get wealth (Deuteronomy 8:18). People tend to misconstrue wealth as meaning only money, or material assets. In fact, wealth is ideas, innovations, inventions which, when done according to the purpose and assignment He has for you in the Earth, bring provision into your life. That power is not going to be in a Power Ball lottery ticket, but in your increased wisdom in solving the problems around you.

As you listen for the Holy Spirit's guidance, He will open your spiritual eyes revealing critical, even life-saving information at just the right time. He directs the right people into your sphere of awareness and influence. He arranges divine appointments and ensures that the wrong doors stay closed and that the right doors become evident and open to you. You will be doing the knocking, and He will be doing the directing.

The Holy Spirit will be your greatest, most effective consultant, and your strongest ally. People will pay a great deal of money for high-powered consultants and analysts to provide their human opinions and educated guesses. You have the very Creator and Architect of the Universe ready and listening for your questions and happy to demonstrate the accurate answers you need in the timing most appropriate. And, He never does anything contrary to the Word of God. He communicates to you what the Father tells Him.

It is exciting to know that you have the very power that created you to lead and guide you into all truth (John 16:13) -- the truth about yourself, your circumstances and your future.

Here is a summary of some of the Holy Spirit's functions directly related to guiding you into your God-ordained purpose:

Holy Spirit's Functions in Helping You Achieve Your Purpose.

- Leader (Romans 8:14)
- Heavenly Language Giver (Acts 2:4)
- Power Giver (Acts 1:8)
- Instruction Giver (Acts 1:2)
- Teacher (Luke 12:12)
- Comforter (John 15:26)
- Speaker of Messages (Mark 13:11)
- Revelator (Luke 2:26)
- Protector (Acts 20:23)
- Advocate (John 14:26)
- Helper of Our Infirmities (Romans 8:26)

Check out each scripture. **Instructor** and **Teacher** are my favorites since the Spirit of the Lord is responsible to get you the information you need to dominate your mountain. You will need to ask Him for the specific areas where you need help. He promises to provide the guidance you need to overcome inevitable challenges and obstacles.

Getting Around Obstacles to Purpose

You can expect that there will be obstacles to achieving your purpose! The job of the Holy Spirit is to *help our infirmities,* which means to *take hold together with against* in the Greek. (Romans 8:26) As you work and **pray in the Spirit,** He joins you to help you achieve what you have been designed to reach and overcome. People will wonder why you are getting as far as you are, accomplishing what you have been assigned to do in record time. He is your invisible, *Secret Helper,* breaking down roadblocks and holding your enemies at bay as you pray and walk in purpose.

That same passage says, "but the Spirit itself [Himself] maketh intercession for us with groanings which cannot be uttered." (Romans 8:26, KJV) When we pray in the Spirit, in our secret heavenly language, we frustrate the demonic forces because they cannot interpret what we are saying to our God, from our recreated spirit to His Spirit. It is a stealthy, uncrackable code which goes into your future to create the necessary resources and situations that propagate the Kingdom of God coming in the Earth, and you achieving your assignment. (See the Appendix for a **Prayer to Receive the Infilling of the Holy Spirit.** Learn how to receive your heavenly language.)

PLANT THE HEAVENS -- YOUR MOUTH SPEAKING GOD'S WORD

Isaiah 51:16 KJV (EMPHASIS ADDED)
And I have put my words in thy mouth, and I have covered thee in the shadow of mine hand, that I may **plant the heavens**, and lay the foundations of the earth, and say unto Zion, Thou art my people.

As you pray in the spirit as a result of the infilling of the Holy Spirit, you play out what is referred to in Isaiah 51:16 as *planting the heavens*. According to the Blue Letter Bible online lexicon, to plant means to establish and set upright so that it is fixed in the ground and taking root. As you speak aloud your prayers, you plant your future with exactly what you will need to be victorious! At the same time you build yourself up (Jude 20) and capability and endurance are increasing.

Practicing His Presence

To go along with this concept of the Holy Spirit being our *Secret Weapon and Guide*, the level of intimacy with Him must increase. He wants us *up close and personal*. We must constantly remind ourselves that the Holy Spirit is with us, acknowledging Him and practicing His presence which enriches the intimacy between you.

He is a gentleman and awaits your invitation to Him into your experience. To learn to hear Him, we must know His voice. That comes with familiarity and frequency. In achieving this intimacy, we must remember to always be God-inside minded. To do this, we must *Practice His Presence*. So, what do I mean by practicing His presence?

I have this habit of visualizing the person of the Holy Spirit sitting in a chair adjacent to mine. Often, when I'm working on a particularly challenging problem, I speak aloud to Him, requesting His guidance and direction. I speak as if I were talking to my very best friend, to someone who really knows me very well. Although I have never heard His voice audibly speaking back to me, He confirms that He hears me in His Word. He always honors His Word.

GOD HEARS YOU

Psalm 4:3 (KJV)
The Lord will hear when I call unto him.

Psalm 5:3 (KJV)
My voice shalt thou hear in the morning, O Lord

Consulting Him, Listening for Him

The Holy Spirit knows you better than anyone else. You can have long conversations with Him and be comforted by the fact that not only does He listen to you, but He provides specific guidance and direction.
I am in the habit of reading the Word of God or some book or work from a respected Christian teacher to gain wisdom and understanding. Without fail, as I tune in for the day, I hear a phrase, a conversation, a TV show that can be captured as an answer to my queries of Him. As long as you have your antennae up, He's broadcasting.

When I find there are limitations in my own understanding, as I try to hear Him more and more clearly, I gain a better and better understanding about my situation.

Be aware that every answer is not immediate. It happens in the course of the day as I go about my daily tasks, even in the ensuing weeks. I could be driving on my way to work, and a thought would occur to me. An idea would come to light. I'll see a person's face who I should call, or recall a book in my personal library that has an answer I need.

I strongly encourage you to always have recording tools of some kind nearby. If I am moving about, I use my phone voice recorder. The same if I am awakened from sleep with an idea. I also record in the Notes feature of my iPhone. Pen and paper should be handy. Use whichever device and process is most effective for you to get those fleeting ideas recorded.

My tendency is toward electronic recording because it is backed up and accessible from anywhere via my smartphone. I enjoy iCloud services, which back up the contents of my phone. As I am developing my work, I typically employ physical and electronic methods. So, I am restful having a safe place to store the ideas and concepts that the Lord gives me.

As I continue along this pathway of learning the Lord's way and hearing His voice, I am maturing in Him. He finds that He can trust me with more and more revelation, more and more insight about my upcoming assignments.

When I look back over my journey, I realize that the journey has helped me to mature, and made me stronger. But, it is indeed a process. It has a definite starting point, but the maturing process never ends. As I move from level to level, I am traveling on a continuum, a Purpose Maturity Continuum.

CHAPTER 4 - THE PURPOSE MATURITY CONTINUUM

PURPOSE MATURITY CONTINUUM: THE FRUIT OF PROGRESS

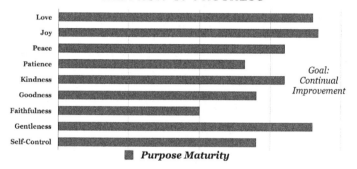

The **Purpose Maturity Continuum**, which is based on Galatians 5:22-25, refers to your level of readiness to assume your God-ordained purpose. I cannot stress enough how important this concept is. If you continue to see the same sites along your journey, and life seems like a merry-go-round with various scenery being repeated, check yourself. Perhaps you are not progressing as you would desire.

**THE FRUIT OF PROGRESS -- THE PURPOSE
MATURITY CONTINUUM**

Galatians 5:22-25 (NLT)
"But the Holy Spirit produces this kind of fruit in
our lives: love, joy, peace, patience, kindness,
goodness, faithfulness, gentleness, and self-
control. There is no law against these things!

A continuum never ends. There are nine aspects of the
Purpose Maturity Continuum. You can always develop
in a category. As these aspects mature, you are
equipped to deal with the situations of life and emerge
victorious. As you progress along your Purpose
Maturity Continuum, you take on the Lord's image.
But, what does He look like? How does that change
you for your purpose?

The presence of the Holy Spirit in your life is for
producing fruit. Fruit means results. That fruit is
exhibited as "love, joy, peace, patience, kindness,
goodness, faithfulness, gentleness, and self control".
(Galatians 5:22-25, KJV) God is helping you to
progress along a continuum where each of these fruits
are increasing as you move through time.

The **Love Category** bands all the maturity categories. It is the power that enables the rest to work. Love is the glue that holds all the maturity aspects together so they can fully function. You can be at various points of maturity on the continuum for each category at any point in time.

LOVE CATEGORY BANDS THE OTHERS

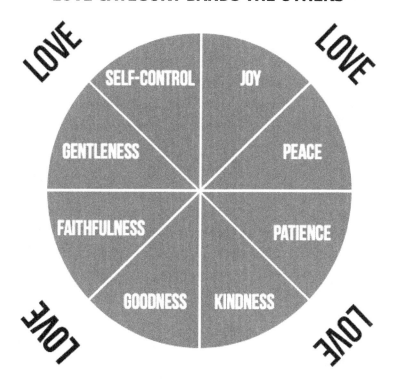

If you were to take stock of your personal progress you might notice that where you are is not where you would like to be. It is the Holy Spirit's mission to help us get to where we need to be to thrive in our purpose and assignments. It is our job to yield to His leading. He speaks to us as we read the scriptures and gain the proper perspective on accurately evaluating where we are along the Purpose Maturity Continuum.

Remember, in Christ no adversity can come through the filter of the Holy Spirit except that it provokes maturing of some aspect of your life in Him. (Romans 8:28) You will experience continual elevation as you proceed through life's tests and trials, as covered in Chapter 2.

There can be multiple tests happening at once in a variety of life areas. You will need to have the necessary character, integrity, and perseverance to experience growth and progress. A plateau is quite possible, as well as demotion if Holy Ghost course corrections and gentle nudges are not heeded.

Let's take an example. God tests us in any of the Galatians 5 characteristics to allow us to see ourselves and our level of development. Suppose you are experiencing a test in the *Love* Continuum. An examination in this area could be when a difficult person gets assigned to your sphere of influence.

Perhaps a co-worker, a boss, or a neighbor is assigned to you. It would be someone in close enough proximity to interact with you on a regular basis. They think it is their sole mission in life to aggravate, frustrate and distress you beyond measure. Somehow, by the Holy Spirit, you are thrown into situation after situation with this person until something changes– either you or them.

You will adjust your attitude and reaction to this annoying individual with the help of the Holy Spirit. This test can go on for months, even years, until finally you have understood what must change about you and your way of handling things.

Wherever you happen to be weak, or in need of development, the Lord arranges tests. When you look back on the situation, you are thankful for His grace and mercy in the situation. You will have either changed or not. If not, expect a repeat exam. It probably will not come in the same format, but, will nevertheless force you to expand and develop in that area. You will proceed upward from level to level in that area, or not. All depends on your willingness. You must desire to progress.

Progressing along the Purpose Maturity Continuum is a lifelong journey. You are more and more capable of handling your assignments. Each hurdle cleared brings you closer and closer to the purpose for which you were designed. It becomes increasingly clearer as you progress that your purpose has a location. Your well-honed talents and gifts fit better in certain places, and specific arenas. As you get to know yourself, you'll find that you function best within certain boundaries and areas.

CHAPTER 5 –
THE SEVEN MOUNTAINS:
LOCATING PURPOSE

The Seven Mountains of Influence

According to a prophecy given to Youth With a Mission founder, Loren Cunningham and Bill Bright, founder of Campus Crusade for Christ, in August 1975, there are seven mountains which are the foundations for every existing society. [ii]And they are listed in the table below:

SEVEN MOUNTAINS OF CULTURAL INFLUENCE:
1. Religion 2. Family 3. Education 4. Government 5. Media and Communications 6. Arts and Entertainment 7. Business and Finance

---

[ii] Hillman, O. (n.d.). *7 cultural mountains*. Retrieved from http://www.7culturalmountains.org

These seven mountains exist as world systems in the global marketplace. The people who control and dominate those mountains, control the nations of the world. As detailed in chapter one, these important concepts have also been explained by Dr. Lance Wallnau, author and founder of the Lance Learning Group. Dr. Wallnau refers to it as the *7M Mandate®*. I'll refer to this concept in the same way.

For more on the Seven Mountains consult *Invading Babylon: The 7 Mountain Mandate* by Dr. Lance Wallnau, and *The Seven Mountain Prophecy: Unveiling the Coming Elijah Revolution* by Johnny Enlow. See also the **Further Reading** Section at the back of the book for more on the Seven Mountains concepts.

Wherever you've chosen to utilize your talents and gifts appears in one or more of these mountains. For example, pastors and evangelists are a part of the *Religion* mountain. Teachers, college professors, trainers and educators work within the *Education* mountain. The basic unit of human relationships is the *Family* nucleus. Not only does the *Family* mountain refer to your belonging to a family at birth and/or being raised by a set of parents, it refers to those individuals who take on professional care giving, as an example, who belong as part of the *Family* mountain.

Politicians, lawyers, and lawmakers are part of the *Government* mountain. Broadcasters, journalists, newspaper publishers, and bloggers are considered part of the *Media and Communications* mountain. Entertainers, sculptors, painters, musicians, and professional athletes belong to the *Arts and Entertainment* mountain.

Bankers, financiers, entrepreneurs and wealth managers are good examples of those in the *Business and Finance* mountain. There are even some professions that pierce several of the mountains, having impact across multiple boundaries. For example lawmakers can impact every mountain.

Let's locate the mountain(s) of your God-ordained purpose using **Exercise #1**.

EXERCISE #1

LOCATE YOUR PRIMARY AND SECONDARY MOUNTAINS
Think about your profession, talents, skills and discern the mountain(s) in which you operate. Your purpose may take you across several of the mountains, but, there is probably a **Primary** and **Secondary** mountain which encompasses the majority of your focus. *(7 Mountains: Religion, Family, Education, Government, Media & Communications, Arts & Entertainment, Business & Finance)*
1. Write your **Primary** and **Secondary** Mountains which fit your current employment. Compare them to where you feel is your purpose.
2. Are they different from what you expected?
3. Who do you know that dominates your mountain?

Your objective is to understand where your true God-ordained purpose is located and to connect with the Holy Spirit to better understand your assignment and the strategy to take your assigned mountain.

Depending on your purpose, you may have a Primary and Secondary Mountain location. For example, writing is my passion, but I work in a corporate environment to focus on my primary means of wealth-building. This indicates Business and Finance as my primary 7M Mandate. Media and Communications is, at this point, secondary. Note that this primary and secondary designation can change as you grow and mature.

So far, we have learned that we are uniquely designed for our God-ordained purpose and that it has a definite location. As we progress, we are being equipped to handle the work God has for us. The layers of our assignment and destiny are being exposed. It becomes more and more evident that proceeding along the road to purpose requires vision and imagination. As the vision becomes clearer, we can see ourselves reaching our destiny.

CHAPTER 6 –
VISION AND IMAGINATION

When Vision and Imagination Intersect

Vision, imagination, and purpose achievement are all interconnected. In its truest sense, vision involves the act of seeing to interpret an image or singular visual picture. Imagination is that ability we humans have to manipulate an image into a shape or format different than its original, so that when done, we can build that final image into a physical work or reality.

As soon as the brain sees and properly interprets the vision of our purpose, we can use our imagination to create that reality. Whether it's a new musical concerto, a highly sought-after business service, or a spectacular basketball move, all are fabricated first in our minds.

The Source of Powerful Imaginations

God has given us the ability to use our imaginations to visualize the solutions to puzzling problems and the will to implement those solutions to make the world a better place. (Genesis 11:5-7) Man has built everything from skyscrapers and information superhighways to micro computer chips and flying cars. Henry David Thoreau, famous American philosopher and poet said, "This world is but a canvas to our imaginations."

In Habakkuk 2:2, the declaration is made to *write the vision* and to make it so abundantly clear that anyone walking by would see it and be impressed enough to take action and carry the message forward to others. When the Lord reveals your purpose vision to you, it's your job to grab it and own it. This is not a casual ownership. It is ownership with the intent to apply and manifest with urgency!

WRITE THE VISION SO EVERYONE CAN SEE IT

Habakkuk 2:2 (KJV)

2 Then the LORD answered me and said:
"Write the vision
And make it plain on tablets,
That he may run who reads it.

Habakkuk 2:2 (The Amplified)

2 And the Lord answered me and said, Write the vision and engrave it so plainly upon tablets that everyone who passes may [be able to] read [it easily and quickly] as he hastens by.

The very act of writing your purpose vision provides the clarity needed to make it manifest. The more clearly you see yourself having fully assumed this future picture of yourself, the greater your excitement and motivation to achieve it.

Imagination Needs Proper Direction

But, our imaginations must be properly harnessed to take the inner visions of our mind's eye from just a mental picture into positive physical reality. Therein lies a potential danger. Man's imagination apart from God can create that which is destructive just as easily as it can create positive change. For example, murder and adultery begin in the mind's eye, just as contemplating a cancer cure or space travel.

Our inner visions must be yielded to the Lord. If not, as noted in Romans 1:21, *vain imaginations* result.

They are idle, worthless thoughts which are of no real consequence, ineffectual and unsuccessful, and the result of a *dark* mind. Alternatively, recognizing and honoring the Lord as God gives the imagination power and light.

VAIN IMAGININGS

Romans 1:21 The Amplified (EMPHASIS ADDED)

21 Because when they knew and recognized Him as God, they did not honor and glorify Him as God or give Him thanks. But instead they became futile and [a] **godless in their thinking** [with vain imaginings, foolish reasoning, and stupid speculations] and their senseless minds were darkened.

The Right Tools: Vision To Reality

Having vivid visions and imaginings without the tools and skills to bring them to fruition is a frustrating experience. With the right tools, you can gain greater clarity and direction from your vision. Take for example, writing the vision down as described in Habakkuk 2:1-3

I think this verse of scripture so aptly describes how a vision board can help us capture our purpose vision in a clear and striking way, so that it captivates the attention of its viewers driving us and others to action.

A purpose vision board can help us to untangle our wrong thinking. It can describe the activities we wish to be doing, or represent the things we'd like to have. By capturing the images of our dreams on the board, they can more readily become part of our physical reality.

The motto I have developed for this use of vision boarding to harness and create the reality of your purpose vision is:

CLARIFY THE VISION, CREATE THE REALITY

In Part 2, you learn the tool kit to create your purpose vision and map out the path to get there. As you proceed through each of the seven steps to creating the life you've been craving, you will gain greater vision clarity. It's an exciting journey and well worth the work.

PART 2:
USING VISION BOARDING
TO MAP YOUR PURPOSE

SEVEN STEPS TO CREATING THE LIFE YOU CRAVE

1. **Imagine** – The formation of a mental picture or vision by capturing thoughts to be harnessed for manifestation through deliberate action.

2. **Write** – Taking harnessed imagination, or vision, and documenting it in a physical medium.

3. **Clarify** – The act of sharpening imagination and vision concepts through review, examination, and analysis.

4. **Map the Pathway** – taking a mental map from the mind to specific action steps required to take a vision to physical reality.

5. **Measure Milestones** – the application of metrics to a plan or vision map which marks the distance to a place you have made up your mind to get to or experience.

6. Be **Accountable** – a person or group to whom you are responsible.

7. **Sustain the Gains** – ensure that moves forward are not followed by regression, digression, divergence, or other movement to a lesser state of maturity and growth.

STEP #1 –
IMAGINE THE PURPOSE VISION

God has given us the ability to capture a thought and harness it to create a vision or image. That is very powerful. It is life-changing when you can take that vision and make it manifest in reality. That is what I am asking you to do with your passions. Your life's goals are associated with images in your mind. In the IMAGINE step, the essence of what you're doing is gathering and constructing the mental images you have of your purpose.

You are to get the images of your passions onto some shareable physical media: a foam-board, a picture journal, or a video. It may be a virtual kaleidoscope of your intentions with your visions all harnessed and tied down in one spot. There you can examine them, analyze them, laugh at them, and cry about them. Then you can easily formulate the plans to bring them into reality.

Here's how you do it.

Where to Start

Get into a creative spot, wherever that might be for you: the beach, an internet café, your home office, or wherever you flow. To get your vision out of your head, you might write individual thoughts on index cards or sticky notes. You could grab images from your favorite virtual websites, like Google Images, iStockPhoto.com, or FreeDigitalPhotos.com, collecting image usage licenses and attribution links as you go along. (See the **Proper Use of Images** Resource at the back of the book.) Place those thoughts and pictures on a foam board or dry erase board so you can arrange them in patterns and categories.

The key is to work quickly. Do not pause. Get the job done. Your purpose vision has already been formulating, especially as you have been reading this book.

Now, pause and take a look at what you have created so far...

You will have a chance to redo, review, and re-imagine. Allow your creative thoughts to flow. In the coming days there may be instances, once you are in that flow, when you get ideas for additions to your creation. Write it down when you think of them. If you can voice record your thoughts, do so. Sometimes those lost thoughts and ideas seem irretrievable once a moment passes. Pray for the Holy Spirit to retrieve ones you think you have forgotten.

Vision-Capture Tools

For vision-capture tools, there are many options. You must find the tools that support your creative energy flow.

- If you enjoy sitting in the middle of your family room floor surrounded by magazines with scissors and glue, do that.

- If you enjoy drawing your own pictures, have a bucket full of crayons, felt tip markers, or colored pencils, then go for it.

There is no right or wrong way. You don't have to be an expert artist to create your purpose vision board. The ultimate objective is for you to have a visual action document of your future.

Your completed vision board is for you to see daily. It is to be kept in a spot where you can glance at it, stare at it, and come up with the scheduled, specific steps to get it done. It should inspire and motivate you. It is there to get you excited, to pump you up about achieving.

Note that some vision boards are high-level, panoramic, and all-encompassing. Some vision boards detail a specific aspect of the overall, high-level purpose vision so you can narrow your focus for a time on a specific aspect of your purpose.

Don't stop at just one vision board. When one reality is achieved, be off creating the next one.

Vision Board Stealth Tactics

Just in case you don't want others to see your vision board, either before, during or after its creation you may need some stealth tactics to limit viewing. The bigger it is, the more ingenuity is required to hide it out.

Whether it is under the bed, or behind the sofa, you should be comfortable that your creative flow will not be disturbed or quenched. This applies if you do not have a personal work space, or if foot traffic will be high where you're working.

When your board is electronic, you can password protect it. That password protection can exist at many levels within your computer system. You can also simply hide your data in the sub-sub folders on your computer's hard drive or cloud backup folder.

Traditional Vision Tools

When I was first introduced to the vision board concept, I only saw **foam board** type examples of vision boards. They were done in various sizes and shapes. **Oak tag paper** was also frequently used since it is flexible and bendable. Whatever the base selected, you can draw your images, or cut and paste photos or magazine pictures easily. Whether simple or elaborate, this approach is tried and true. Purpose visions can also be captured in a **journal** or a **scrapbook**. "What's the difference?" you may ask.

A **journal** is a bound, lined or unlined book of pages. The journal could be used to house your hand-drawn pictures or photographs. Also, journals are used to record daily thoughts and feelings as you walk toward your purpose. I have journaled for many years and have boxes full of completed ones compiled over the years. Journaling for me is cathartic in nature, a place where I can dump ideas without the constraints of a specific format or objective. Journaling can be used to get random thoughts and current interests as well.

One of my other favorite traditional vision-achievement tools is the **scrapbook**. A scrapbook is traditionally a bound collection of photographs, pictures and newspaper clippings which are gathered for preservation's sake.

Now, craft stores like Michael's or Hobby Lobby's have entire sections dedicated to scrapbooking materials. Pre-cut words, backgrounds, and various weighted papers can be used to design custom images. If you are one who loves to be able to touch and feel your dreams when you review them, then this physical medium is a great option. There is nothing like having physical pages to turn. Each page is its own vision and work of art.

The scrapbook can be themed and categorized. A single subject matter can be covered in a single scrapbook, or multiple areas can be covered. The completed physical book can be neatly shelved and pulled out to view. They make wonderful keepsakes which can be passed down the family generations. You can even photograph the scrapbook pages and later store them with your digital photos.

The key is remain focused on the objective: to look at your current book often. Allow the pictures to direct you to your God-ordained destiny and purpose.

High-Tech vs. Not So

When you have multiple images to store, you may need a physical portfolio case. For digital media, there are also electronic portfolios and creation software with which you can experiment.

Here are some suggestions:

- For photo sharing: Facebook, Shutterfly, SmugMug, Flickr, PhotoBucket, Dropbox
- For video media sharing: YouTube, Vimeo, Instagram, Ustream
- For online media creation: Animoto, Prezi, WeVideo

These sites have both free and low cost options depending on the level of features you prefer. Animoto has an iPhone app where you can access your material from your phone. Animoto and Prezi combine digital photos and videos in a unique and colorful way. They use technology to optimize your digital media and integrate it with a pre-formatted set of template selections and music. The end product can be uploaded to YouTube, Facebook or Instagram to be shared with friends, family or clients. So now you have both traditional and digital media choices.

One word of caution: it is very important to back up your digital information. Try using Dropbox.com as a means of storing electronic media. There are both free and paid plans available depending on the number of gigabytes of storage needed. It's well worth the effort to avoid losing your hard work.

The Value of Digital Media

So, what is the value of using digital media? A personalized video containing images you've designed also directs your thoughts to where you are going. What you will achieve is of great impact. Using a **purpose vision video** is like programming your thoughts to higher and higher realms.

When you change your thoughts, you can change the words you speak; when you change the words you speak, you change your actions and get where you were designed to go. When combining video (moving images) with your affirming spoken words declaring your future into existence, you have a power-packed tool to use. It can be made portable and played as often as you like. For example, in the morning before you get out of the house, on your public transit commute, as you take a walk in the afternoon... you can play your purpose vision video anytime and anywhere, especially from your smart phone device which you can carry along with you.

You can choose any or all of these options. What is exciting is that there are multiple options. Wherever your creative flow is greatest is what you should use. *But, choose the tool kit with which you can be consistent.*

STEP #2 –

WRITE THE PURPOSE VISION

Step#1 helps you gather the images of your purpose vision and explains the tools that can be used. The point of **Step#2** is to write your purpose vision into words. Writing it out helps to clarify it in your mind. Our motto is:

CLARIFY THE VISION, CREATE THE REALITY

Once you get the images out of your head and down on some media form in Step #1, you can be free to analyze and ferret out your design and purpose. The very action of writing your multi-layered revelation down begins a flow of creative energy. Seeing your key points out on paper provide the insight you will need to see patterns, connect events and identify mistakes, past and impending. You'll be encouraged by how far you've come. At the same time, you'll see how far you must go.

The framework we're going to build upon is the **Talent Grid**. The Talent Grid is a simple device that will help you get started by building awareness of your divine design. Your **talents**, **passions**, **likes** and **dislikes** point the way to exactly what your God-ordained purpose is. The following exercise will guide your creative energy.

Get a sheet of blank paper. Draw a vertical and horizontal line evenly dividing the sheet into four quadrants. Label each quadrant as follows: Upper Left "Talents"; Upper Right "Passions"; Lower Left "Likes"; and Lower Right "Dislikes". (You'll see this again in **Exercise #3** at the end of this chapter.) Let's first explain each quadrant.

The Talent Focus

Talent is defined as any employable skill you may have for which you might receive pay. For example, you might be able to repair computers. You may be an elementary school teacher, or sell insurance. Or, you may be an airline pilot and have the skill of flying different types of airplanes. There are certain talents you have that aid you in doing your skill.

As an example, an airline pilot would likely be talented in the following:

- **Communicating** personably with passengers and co-workers;
- **Deciding** quickly, with accuracy and precision;
- **Solving problems** with quick understanding of numerical concepts;
- **Estimating** from numerical information;
- **Sensing spatial** relationship intuitively; and
- **Reading and interpreting** flight instruments

Now to you. What are you good at? Think of past jobs you have had. Write them in the *Talents* space. Then write out the talents you possess which allow you to successfully perform those skills, such as the airline pilot example above. Write your talent ideas in the upper left quadrant.

The Passions Focus

Move to the upper right-hand quadrant. Here you are going to list your **Passions**. A passion is something you would do whether you get paid for it or not. Some examples might be collecting vintage Marvel comic books, or playing the saxophone in a band, or rock climbing. These are the activities that make you smile. You have to arrange to do more of these passion activities.

Likes and Dislikes Hone Your Direction

You would not ordinarily think that something so elementary as what you **Like** or **Dislike** has something to do with your purpose. For everything from the food you eat and your allergies, to the people you naturally connect with or are repulsed by, it is part of your Divine Design. If you are a "polar bear" and enjoy the freezing cold weather, that will determine what geographical location to which you are drawn. A "polar bear" person living in the middle of a hot, muggy climate like the Houston, Texas might make for an uncomfortable time.

In the work environment, you may truly dislike a micro-managing boss when you're used to being allowed the freedom to use your creative energy to develop and implement. If you are a very creative person, stiff and stodgy corporate cultures may not be your cup of tea.

So, in the lower half of the Talent Grid, list your likes and dislikes. Everything from the food you eat, to the climates you enjoy, to the people with whom you enjoy working.

Some Categories for Likes and Dislikes

Food	Gadgets
Climate	Toys
Hobbies	Cars
Movies	Travel
Personalities	Clothing and Fashion
TV shows	Furniture

Value of the Talent Grid

Let's take a look at what is indicated by the talent grid. You may be wondering about the value of such an exercise and what it may have to do with your God-ordained purpose.

Your purpose has already been established. It is up to you to recognize and nurture it. You could already be walking in it and not recognize that fact. Or, you may have been searching for a job which fits your academic credentials or because you need a paycheck, but, that job uses few of your gifts, talents and passions. How tragic it would be for you to continue in that vein and not change course and head toward the purpose for which you were designed.

Do you see any patterns? Write them down as you recognize them.

Now, ask yourself the series of questions in **Exercise #2.** This will be the pre-work for **Exercise #3.**

EXERCISE #2

COMPLETING THE TALENT GRID: QUESTIONS TO ASK YOURSELF
1. What have I always been good at?
2. What have people always complimented me on and why?
3. What service was I rendering when I received that compliment?
4. What of these activities makes me smile when I'm doing them?
5. Which of the activities make me feel engaged and happy?
6. When did I feel most at home and why?

Your Task This Week: As you go about your daily activities this week, immediately write down the activities that you enjoy most. Catch yourself laughing or smiling. Take a mental snapshot of you in the middle of that activity. Write it down on your talent grid. You can even pull out the old high-school yearbook, or dust off some old photos of days gone by.

Relive the moments that brought you delight. You will start to really see why you are here and why you are important. This is the stuff of purpose. It will become clearer and clearer.

You will notice that when you are doing what you were born to do, designed to do, there is a flow. You may not be perfect at it, but it fits you. Capturing those moments is your daily task. Then ask yourself the question:

How Can I Be Doing More of Those Purpose Ideas in My Career?

Find out if there is a career or company that would allow you to do your purpose vision and get paid for it. Determine whether there is a company you can create yourself or form a partnership that would support you as you do more of your God-ordained purpose.

Be aware up front that this is an iterative process. Even after you get this version completed, expect to refresh it frequently. You are not stagnant. Your situation is not stagnant. All is fluid and changing around you. You must be self-aware and constantly listening for the Holy Spirit's update on what you can do to move further in achieving your purpose vision.

It is an exciting process, is it not?

Now, create your vision board with all the information you have gathered from your Talent Grid using the instructions in **Exercise #3**. Use the example that follows it as a guide. *This is your first purpose vision board!* Review it and marvel.

EXERCISE #3
THE TALENT GRID

TALENTS	PASSIONS
LIKES	DISLIKES

Directions:

1. Write down as many ideas as you can for each of the four categories.

2. Draw pictures on the reverse side of this sheet of paper to represent the key element of each quadrant. I encourage you to do lots of free hand drawings whether you feel you are good at it or not.

3. See the Completed Talent Grid Vision Board Example. It combines the results of **Exercise #1** in Chapter 5 on the location of your purpose in the Seven Mountains with the Talent Grid.

COMPLETED TALENT GRID
VISION BOARD EXAMPLE
(with 7 Mountains Locations)

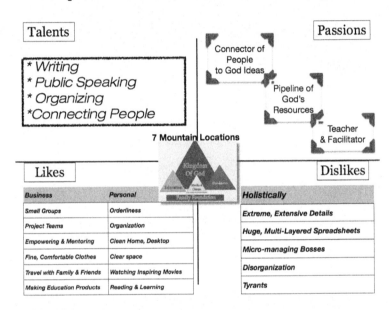

Talents
* Writing * Public Speaking * Organizing *Connecting People

Connector of People to God Ideas

Pipeline of God's Resources

Passions

Teacher & Facilitator

7 Mountain Locations

Likes		Dislikes

Business	Personal	Holistically
Small Groups	Orderliness	Extreme, Extensive Details
Project Teams	Organization	Huge, Multi-Layered Spreadsheets
Empowering & Mentoring	Clean Home, Desktop	Micro-managing Bosses
Fine, Comfortable Clothes	Clear space	Disorganization
Travel with Family & Friends	Watching Inspiring Movies	Tyrants
Making Education Products	Reading & Learning	

STEP #3 –
CLARIFY THE VISION:
YOUR PURPOSE TIMELINE

The next vision board project you will complete is the **Purpose Vision Timeline**. This powerful exercise is the methodology we will use to demonstrate the following:

- How far you have come up to this point in your life.
- What the **SEs (Significant Events)** you have experienced in your life have wrought in you and how they have prepared you for your future.
- Circumstances where you have thrived and flourished, or just survived and even diminished in capacity.
- People to whom you have been drawn and what they have taught you, both positive and negative.
- Who you were being at that juncture in your life? Empowered? Full of Life? Tired? Weary? Confused?

Follow the instructions listed below **Exercise#4**. Think of each **SE** as a *time slice* of your life to be examined in this exercise.

EXERCISE #4
THE PURPOSE TIMELINE: SIGNIFICANT EVENTS

Category	Time Slice#1	Time Slice#2	Time Slice#3	Time Slice#4...
Event Name?				
What Year?				
Physical Location?				
Key People?				
Who Were You Being?				

© 2013 – Shawn R McLeod

Gather the following materials:
- Sticky notes
- Pen, markers
- Portable dry erase board or foam board

Think of at least four SEs which have impacted you personally. It could be a personal or family event, or it could be a career-related event. This is something that could have been particularly joyous, tragic, hurtful, or traumatic. Some examples might be: you got fired from a job, someone close to you dies, you had your first child/grandchild, and so on.

Complete the Significant Event time slices as follows writing your individual thoughts on a single sticky note:

- **Event Name?** Significant Event Name. First job at Company *X*, University as a Teen, Grandfather's Death. *PINK STICKY*

- **What Year?** List the year when this SE occurred. (e.g., 1993, 2010, 2012) BLUE STICKY. Physical Location? Where you were when this SE occurred. (e.g., San Francisco, CA at the house where I grew up; Kraft Foods as a CIO, Cranbury, NJ) *BLUE STICKY*

- **Key People?** People who were with you during this SE. They may have helped you in a big way, or they may have contributed to harming you. List their name or the initials of their name. (John Smith, or J.S.) *PURPLE STICKY*

- **Who were you being?** What state were you in emotionally, and from a maturity view point. *YELLOW STICKY*

- **What was the Lord showing you about yourself and your environment?** *GREEN STICKY*

Here's How to Place Your Multi-colored Sticky Notes Vertically for Each SignificantEvent (SE) Time Slices.

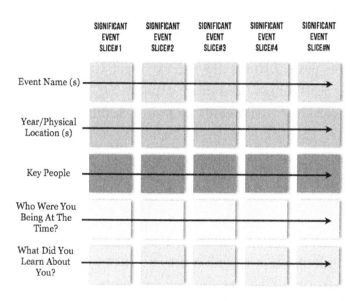

Purpose Timeline Pattern Recognition Charts.

As you review each SE side-by-side, you will notice changes in your behavior and attitude resulting from those SEs and the people with whom you associated during that time in your life. Imagine that those gifts and talents you exhibited are threads throughout the fabric of your life. They point you toward your purpose and help you to see more clearly.

As you pass through the SEs you get tougher, more resilient, stronger, and more capable. Or, perhaps you discover your weaknesses and your Achilles heel. You will see that some of those events have taken you in the wrong direction, and that you may have to take steps to recover.

Feel free to draw pictures and symbols to represent the various aspects of your journey, your gifts, and your talents. You can also use internet resources. See the Resource Pages at the end of this book with links to image resources as well as instructions regarding the proper use and crediting to observe copyrights and licensing requirements.

As you detail these thoughts and feelings you will reflect on where you are now and what comes to light about your life's purpose. You will start to see how you have always used certain skills and talents. There will be elements of your personality, both positive and negative that always rise to the surface and combine to propel you towards your destiny.

Analysis and Pattern Recognition

Analyze any patterns you see that occurred during your SEs. Has a business, or a ministry been birthed from these experiences? Did your experience good or bad, help someone else? Did your mental toughness increase or decrease? Did you feel stronger, or more capable after the event? Did a sense of panic rule?

PURPOSE TIMELINE PATTERN RECOGNITION

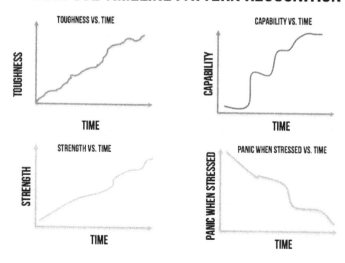

STEP #4 –
MAP THE PATHWAY
TO YOUR PURPOSE VISION

The **Quarterly Purpose Vision Project Chart** in **Exercise #5** is the tool that you will use to illustrate the pathway to your purpose vision in an overview format. It should include major milestones and sub-tasks to be accomplished. This project chart illustrates your action schedule, including what you will do and when you plan to complete it. As you drill down, the chart will include start and finish dates for individual tasks or events.

The advantages of this form are that you can:

- See a full year at once.
- See parallel vs. serial task relationships.
- Get a sense for how long it may take to accomplish this portion of your vision.
- Tape two forms together side-by-side to increase space and consolidate two years on one sheet.

EXERCISE #5:
QUARTERLY PURPOSE VISION PROJECT CHART

Purpose Pathway for Year - (YYYY):			
Purpose Project Description:			
Major Milestones: 1. _____ 2. _____ 3. _____ 4. _____			
Action Step Overview by Quarter			
	Q 1	Q 2	Q 3	Q 4
Action #1:				
Action #2:				
Action #3:				
Action #4:				
Resource Needs				

Consider this Quarterly Purpose Vision Project Chart as a big-picture document to which you will later add the details in a natural progression toward your purpose vision. Later in the **Monthly Timeline to Action** in **Exercise #6** of Step #5 is where you really add detail to the milestones to be accomplished as you move toward your dreams.

STEP #5 –
SET YOUR MILESTONES:
MEASURE SMARTER

Once you have mapped the pathway to your purpose you have to create visual mile markers along the road way. This creates focus points on the way to achieving the completed goal. Breaking up the distance between you and a final achievement will ensure you don't lose heart along the way. Having a tool to measure your progress helps avoid stalls in the future.

Construct the Detail Plan

Your Quarterly Purpose Project Chart in **Exercise #5** is the high-level view of your direction. You can use several sheets of the form to map a timeframe needing multiple years. You can see how all the pieces fit together. At the same time, you can dive into one area or aspect of a single goal and its milestones. With the more detailed focus, you can figure out how to interject the achievement of purpose into your day to day activities.

Chart Your Progress

To measure your progress is to create a means at the start that allows you to check up on yourself. You can also use this as a tool in explaining to your accountability partners where you are. It contains dates describing when something is to be accomplished and the resources needed in advance.

Analyze What Needs to Change

The best laid plans can go awry. When you or your partners notice something is going *out of whack,* stop. Take the time to figure out where you have veered off course. Enact your course corrections. Perhaps your original imaginings of how things were to go were incorrect. Revisit your assumptions. Recalculate the necessary adjustments and their costs.

The concept of the S.M.A.R.T.E.R. vision goals has been around for a very long time. It is not broken, so we need not modify the idea, but, employ it as a useful tool.

S – Specific
M – Measurable
A – Achievable
R – Realistic
T – Time-bound
E – Evaluatable
R – Re-do and Repeat the cycle

As you dwell on the visions God has given you which point toward your true purpose, there will be specific tasks you will be given to accomplish. As you discover them, write them down, being as SPECIFIC and detailed as possible. Draw pictures, words, and whatever else makes sense.

Then, quantify what is to be completed, for example number of pounds lost, or number of pages written. That is **SPECIFIC** and **MEASURABLE.**

The goals you will be setting as you achieve your purpose certainly must be **ACHIEVABLE** and **ATTAINABLE.** Stretch goals are one thing, but placing a demand upon yourself that is not achievable and realistic is disheartening and depressing. However, they should require you to extend beyond the comfortable.

As you write out these specific tasks, you assign a **REALISTIC** timeframe for completion. The task should be **TIME-BOUND**. For example, you can say, "By this week", "By this time next year", "By my 50th birthday, I will have completed...".

EVALUATE, RE-DO and **REPEAT THE CYCLE** are what continually breathe new life into your vision. Re-look at it. Re-imagine it. Repeating this cycle as each assignment is completed refreshes the marching orders and gives new life to your mission.

Recognize Accomplishments

This is one of the most important steps. Use a journal or photos to record your progress against your milestones. Decide in advance how you might reward yourself and your team members. Small or large recognition, decide what you want to recognize and what is appropriate. Then go for it!

EXERCISE #6:
MONTHLY TIMELINE TO ACTION

Purpose Pathway Month - (MM/YYYY):			
Monthly Purpose Milestone:			
Action Step Detail by Week			
Week 1			
Week 2			
Week 3			
Week 4/5			
Partner's Task: 1. 2. 3.			
Resource Needs:			
Notes:			

STEP #6 –
SEEK ACCOUNTABILITY PARTNERS

Pray In Midwives: Birthers of Vision

Once you have mapped out your purpose and the goals associated with it, you can easily see the distance between where you are now and where you want to be. You quickly realize you may need some help. It is very important to know you are not alone on the pathway to achievement of purpose. The right partners become an invaluable help in birthing your vision. They could be thought of as midwives in your vision delivery.

Midwifery is no lost art. There is a definite spiritual application. According to the Merriam Webster online dictionary it is defined as the "art, act, or process of producing, bringing forth, or bringing about". In choosing a midwife, consider the following:

Characteristics of a Midwife:

Personality	Meshes with yours Desires the best for you Not jealous
Function	Skilled in the area of expertise needed
	Excites your creativity Motivates You
	Intercedes on your behalf Provide alternative perspectives Calls you on bad behavior

The Lord arranges divine connections and appointments to bring your midwife into your sphere of influence. In your midwife of the hour, you find a kindred spirit, someone who has a similar or complementary burden on their hearts.

There are seasons for midwives in your life. You might expect that once your vision is birthed, you no longer have a connection. Then it is on to the next project or assignment. You cannot hold onto what the Lord gives for a specific timeframe. Sometimes you have a lifetime connection. Be prepared for either event.

When you're together, your goals and personalities seem to mesh. They want the best for you and you for them. Often, you have something in you that they need to birth their vision, and they have something you will need. It is often an exchange of creative energy.

A vision that the Lord gives arrives much like the birth of a human child. There is a time or season when it is due for delivery. There can be a premature delivery as well as an overdue birth.

Called at the moment of imminent delivery, the midwife guides the child from the mother's womb with a steady hand. The birth canal can be a very narrow space.

The pushing, sweat, blood, tears, undignified grunts, screams, and pants will occur, especially on difficult deliveries. The child can get stuck on the descent if not in the right position and posture. The Holy Spirit is the overseer for all involved, guiding the activities to their success. So too the accomplishing of your purpose vision.

The vision not only has a time element, but takes up space, has impact and influence. However, it requires a series of pushes to get it out. When it's close to coming to fruition, you can experience contractions and birth pains.

When you're close to delivery things often get increasingly difficult, even seemingly impossible. It seems that one obstacle after another blocks your pathway. This time is crucial and without perseverance, the series of pushes required if not endured, result in a failed vision delivery.

The larger the vision, the larger the push required. It is also very possible that multiple midwives, skilled in a variety of areas are needed to bring the vision to pass. Delivery takes patience and dedication.

Acquire Purpose Accountability Partners

Another accountability concept I want to introduce is the *Purpose Accountability Partner*, or PAP. This Purpose Accountability Partner and the midwife can be one in the same person, but, they may not be. You can agree on goals along the pathway to your purpose. You establish goals up front which you plan to meet. Then, you can motivate one another toward the progress needed to achieve those goals.

You can regularly check in with this individual. The objective would be to keep you honest about achieving your goals in the quality and timing that you have set forth as a goal. They can ask you the tough questions you might not ask yourself. They can provide suggestions and recommendations. For example, you may decide that your personal longevity is a serious goal. You can find a PAP who may have a similar goal. As the two of you walk forward you encourage and motivate one another. It is not absolutely necessary to have similar or same goals, but, it helps if you are pulling in the same direction.

Meet Regularly

I highly recommend that you plan to connect with your midwife(s) and/or purpose accountability partner(s) regularly. You can decide on the regularity up front. The group can get together with calendars and settle on meeting frequency and duration.

Whenever purpose is to be birthed, things will get in the way. Life will find multiple reasons to divert you. You will need to remain focused on the end point and keep putting one foot in front of the other, marching inexorably to the end of your present assignment.

STEP #7 –
SUSTAIN THE GAINS

When you look back on the time and effort you have spent in birthing your God-ordained purpose, you will want to tenaciously hold onto what you have gained. It will feel so good to get where you're going, but then there will be other new challenges which lie ahead. The danger is in sliding backward, not holding onto the foundation you have built.

So, how can we *Sustain the Gains?* Much of this book has stressed writing your vision down. You must write and rewrite your vision, especially as new dreams and revelation come to light. You must not sit still and rest on your laurels. There is always more to do for the Kingdom of God.

Set up time with your accountability partners. Check in on how they have been doing against their established goals of achieving purpose. Break out the old copies of your written plans. In whatever format you have archived them, take them out to review them. Rethink them.

When you look at something you wrote a year ago or more, you will be amazed and encouraged by your progress. Revel in that feeling if only for a short time. Now let's start **Exercise #7**.

EXERCISE #7

STEPS FOR SUSTAINING THE GAINS
1. Relook at your written purpose and goals.
2. Determine what you may have missed, if anything.
3. Rewrite, adjust, and update them for your current status and intentions.
4. Construct a timeline along with the steps to achieve what you may have missed, or new goals toward achieving new assignments of purpose.
5. Re-establish, restore, and reactivate your accountability relationships.
6. Pray for and obtain new accountability partners for the next vision and assignment.
7. Design reward(s) to acknowledge your progress, small or large.
8. Assess you battle readiness or weariness and plan for rest as needed.

Some of the targets looked impossible, but, nevertheless God honored your faithfulness and diligence.

Some items you may have missed or de-prioritized for a different time period in your life. Other areas you may have discovered were not on target after all. Sort through it. Categorize and assign timeframes for the goals you plan to continue to pursue.

As you look forward you may need to reactivate your mastermind group. Prayer about divine connections and appointments is a necessity. Maintain your intimacy with God via the Holy Spirit who will continually guide you into all truth.

I cannot overemphasize the importance of staying connected to the True Vine which is Jesus Christ. He will be your dependable source of continued revelation and direction.

PART 3:
KEY RESOURCES

FAQ'S:
FREQUENTLY ASKED QUESTIONS

Common Methodology Questions

Some of the questions we encounter regarding the methodology in this book are listed below. This is not advice, but, food for thought. In every situation, you should bring your questions first to the Lord. He will always answer.

What if I'm *unequally yoked* in marriage and my spouse does not share my purpose vision?

> Pray for the Lord's direction about the part you play in helping your spouse achieve his/her calling. Set aside time for creating your vision of where you feel the Lord is leading you both individually and as a couple. I Corinthians 7:10-11 (MSG) says "And if you are married, stay married. This is the Master's command, not mine."

How do I work on achieving my purpose when most of my time is spent with my *spouse and children* at this point in my life?

Ministry begins at home. Part of your God-ordained purpose is to help both your spouse and children to achieve their individual purposes, as well as your corporate purpose as a family. Purpose achievement is a generational concept. That being said, don't lose sight of your desires. Work on them in the time you can devote. Circumstances can change as time proceeds. Kids get older and more independent. Spouses will need to learn to work together in helping each other achieve purpose.

Suppose I am *retired* and feel my age is beyond the point of finding my purpose?

Your retirement is another opportunity to reinvent yourself. Both pre-retirement and post-retirement planning require vision. Use the Purpose Vision Timeline as a tool to rediscover what makes you smile. You are in a perfect position to help others achieve their purpose as well, since you may have more time now than when you were working.

What if I'm *too scared* to live in my purpose?

2 Tim 1:7 says, "For God hath not given us the spirit of fear; but of power, and of love, and of a sound mind." That fear of living your purpose is not coming from God. Find some *fear not*

scriptures in the bible on which to meditate. The phrase *fear not* is mentioned so many times in the bible because God knew we would be susceptible to it. Check out these great *Fear Not* Examples: Joshua 1:9; Matthew 10:29-31; Hebrew 13:5-6.

How can I achieve my purpose vision if my current job takes up all my time and energy?

One of your vision boards could entail how you can better manage and conserve your time to allow greater focus on purpose.

You've read this Book and you're still not sure where to *start*?

Start with completing the exercises. Not only will they be fun, but, you will learn something about yourself you had not thought about before. Choose a partner to work with on your purpose discovery journey.

Why should I push myself? It's easier to live an ordinary life.

It depends on how you define *easy*. If you are unhappy where you are, it's an indicator that it is time to rediscover what brings you fulfillment. Using the exercises in this book can help with that.

How can I transition from living as I do now to living my purpose without experiencing income loss?

The Lord liberates the resources needed to fund His projects. Seek Him first for His purpose plans and strategies. Second, don't undervalue your current experiences. They may be helping you hone the skills you will need as you move further along your purpose vision timeline. Third, create a financial budget plan which will allow you to create the nest egg you will need. You can create a vision board for this as well.

Proper Use of Internet Images

When constructing vision boards a reliable source for digital images is often requested. Google Images is a frequently used resource for photos or graphics. Were you aware that images are original works of authorship and are covered by copyright laws as established under the protection of the U.S. Constitution? Those laws were created to manage the use of images, among other things, by those other than their owners. The objectives are to ensure users respect the owner's rights and also to provide some terms for their use.

Did you know that copyright protection exists even if an author does not file any official paperwork? Yes, it is true. But, copyright filing is required to allow authors to enforce their rights. You should also know that acknowledging the source of an image when you use it is not the same as gaining permission to use it.

Also, copyright information can be embedded into the source code for a digital image. Snagging and pasting without express permission can lead to Digital Millennium Copyright Act enforcement activity.

Fair Use guidelines have been established which provide a framework for when and how images can be used. But, observing these guidelines is not a guarantee that you cannot be sued. Attribution, or giving the owner credit somehow when you use it, does not make its use *ok*.

Copyright Law of the United States defines the factors of *Fair Use* in Section 107 for when the work is used under any of following conditions:

> "(1) the purpose and character of the use, including whether such use is of a commercial nature or is for nonprofit educational purposes;
> (2) the nature of the copyrighted work;
> (3) the amount and substantiality of the portion used in relation to the copyrighted work as a whole; and
> (4) the effect of the use upon the potential market for or value of the copyrighted work."

When in doubt, consult a copyright attorney or use resources which provide free images with licensing. Follow the stated licensing rules for each image used.

So, what is the process you should follow to allow use of an image from the internet? You will need to:

Know before you use!

Determine the source of the image, then determine if they will grant a license for use, or if it is public domain. (*Public domain* means that the image is no longer covered by copyright.)

If a license is available, follow the guidelines established by that license, including paying a fee if it is required, and follow any of the stated rules for use. Keep the documentation for later use as proof you have followed the proper procedures.

With all that said, there is the **Creative Commons**, (CC), licensing concept, which encourages sharing of various works via the internet in a legal way that are not as restrictive as copyright. CC uses a selection of standardized licenses which preserves the author's rights in a way that they choose, but, provides guidelines to a potential user as to how the work should be shared. For more information on Creative commons Licenses please refer to this link:

Creative Commons Website
http://creativecommons.org/licenses/

So, where are these elusive images that are safe for you to use in your work? Here is a non-exhaustive list that I've gathered which should get you started.

Image Links:

http://istockphoto.com
http://pdphoto.org/
http://Corbis.com/
http://MorgueFile.com/
http://FreeDigitalPhotos.net/
http://ShutterStock.com/
http://Thinkstock.com/
http://flickr.com/creativecommons/

Various government entities also offer resources for images:

The National Oceanic and Atmospheric Administration (NOAA) has a great library of water photos.

http://photolib.noaa.gov/

The U. S. Fish and Wildlife Service offers images.

http://images.fws.gov/

SUMMARY

In reading this book, working through the exercises and completing your vision boards you have learned how to clarify your God-ordained purpose vision. This is just a starter-kit. Vision development is a constant process requiring renewal and refreshing. As you change, the boards, scrapbooks, journals and videos can be updated.

Seek out and maintain your mastermind Purpose Accountability Partnerships and build new relationships as you are led by the Holy Spirit. Stay encouraged! Adversity will indeed come. Stay connected to the Lord. Your God-ordained purpose cannot be achieved without your constant consulting from the Spirit of God. Include your purpose vision projects in your monthly calendar and in your monthly budget.

Above all, observe yourself. When you catch yourself smiling while doing your day-to-day tasks, write it down in your journal. It's either confirmation of the self discovery work you've already done, or indicating something to be added.

Continue in Him and remember our motto:

CLARIFY THE VISION, CREATE THE REALITY

PURPOSE PRAYERS

Salvation Prayer

Pray this aloud:

Father, according to Romans 10:9-10, I come to you in the name of Jesus Christ your Son. I acknowledge that He died on the cross for my sins and that He was buried and rose from the dead. I accept Jesus as my personal savior, that He may become Lord of my life.

Amen!

This is an act of faith. Now tell someone of your new relationship with Christ. Ask the Lord to lead you to a Bible-believing, loving fellowship and join their assembly. Attend regularly. Read your Bible asking the Holy Spirit to open your understanding. You will grow and mature in your spiritual life as you continue in Him.

May the Lord richly bless you!

Receiving the Infilling of the Holy Spirit

There is an experience beyond salvation called the infilling of the Holy Spirit. Upon receiving salvation, your spirit is recreated and is brand new. The Holy Spirit can then come into your spirit and dwell there. However, according to Acts 2:1-4, there is a continual filling that is promised. It is not complicated. It is biblical. It happens as soon as you have believed it to be so.

Acts 2:1-4

2 And when the day of Pentecost was fully come, they were all with one accord in one place.

2 And suddenly there came a sound from heaven as of a rushing mighty wind, and it filled all the house where they were sitting.

3 And there appeared unto them cloven tongues like as of fire, and it sat upon each of them.

4 And they were all filled with the Holy Ghost, and began to speak with other tongues, as the Spirit gave them utterance.

This promise is demonstrated in you as you speak aloud in tongues as the Holy Spirit aids you. In the same way you received salvation, you can receive the gift of the infilling of the Holy Spirit evidenced by speaking in tongues, your spiritual language. This gift you utilize in your daily prayer life and throughout the day as you need strength and wisdom for the tasks at hand.

This building up of your spirit man is written in Jude 1:20, where it describes the building up process. As you speak in tongues in your holy prayer language, your understanding is disengaged. The Holy Spirit through your speaking aloud is creatively establishing mysteries into the spirit realm, effectively planting the heavens with resources and empowerment to reveal and help you achieve His purpose for you.

WE NEED TO CONSTANTLY BUILD UP OUR RECREATED SPIRITS

Jude 1:20-21

20 But ye, beloved, building up yourselves on your most holy faith, praying in the Holy Ghost,
21 Keep yourselves in the love of God, looking for the mercy of our Lord Jesus Christ unto eternal life. (Emphasis Added)

FURTHER READING

(1) *Change Agent: Engaging Your Passion to Be the One Who Makes a Difference,* by Os Hillman. Charisma House: 2011.

(2) *The Gift in You: Discover New Life Through Gifts Hidden in Your Mind,* by Dr. Caroline Leaf. Thomas Nelson Publishers: 2009.

(3) *Invading Babylon: The 7 Mountain Mandate,* by Lance Wallnau, Bill Johnson. Destiny Image Publishers, Inc.: 2013.

(4) *Invading the Seven Mountains with Intercession: How to Reclaim Society Through Prayer,* by Tommi Femrite. Charisma House: 2011.

(5) *The Seven Mountain Mantle: Receiving the Joseph Anointing to Reform Nations,* by Johnny Enlow. Creation House: 2009.

(6) *The Seven Mountain Prophecy: Unveiling the Coming Elijah Revolution,* by Johnny Enlow. Creation House: 2008.

ABOUT SHAWN R. MCLEOD

Shawn R. McLeod has always been passionate about helping women find and walk in their God-ordained purpose. Her delight is to teach others the principles of achieving that purpose by harnessing one's imagination and vision. Her goal is to help Christian women have a greater impact in the world through building their inner vision of themselves dominating in their mountain of influence.

She is a wife and mother, and knows what it means to balance career and family. As a native of Pennsylvania, Shawn graduated from Drexel University's B.S. and M.S. Engineering programs. While working in Global Supply Chain Management in the healthcare industry, Shawn obtained her M.B.A. from Strayer University.

As a motivational speaker and author, Shawn takes the life-changing message of *Living Your Purpose* on the road to share with as many people as possible. She uses her website LivingYourPurpose.org to reach a global audience. Shawn is a past district officer and current club officer in her local Toastmasters International Public Speaking club. She specializes in

Technical Writing, Speech Writing, and Business Writing.

Also, through her blog at 10TalentWealth.com, she creates and shares practical tips and manuals for personal money management, as well. She works with the women's ministry in her church on marketing and event promotion. You can contact Shawn at:

Email: Shawn@LivingYourPurpose.org

Book Order Form

The Ultimate Guide to Living Your Purpose:
7 Steps to Creating the Life You Crave

☐ Yes, I want _____ copies at $19.95 each plus $4 shipping per book. Applicable state tax will be added.

FAX ORDER TO:
888-550-9525
EMAIL QUESTIONS TO:

Shawn@LivingYourPurpose.org

Yes, charge my: ☐ AmEx ☐ VISA ☐ Discover, or ☐ Master Card

Name:

Address:

City, State, Zip::

Contact Phone #:

Email Address:

Credit Card #: _____-_____-_____-_____

Expiration Date: (MM/YY): _____/_____

Security Code: _____

Signature:_____

CPSIA information can be obtained
at www.ICGtesting.com
Printed in the USA
BVOW03s2121060217
475464BV00003B/6/P